Thirty Days in L

in 1919

Peter Saurusaitis

Alpha Editions

This edition published in 2023

ISBN : 9789357949507

Design and Setting By
Alpha Editions
www.alphaedis.com
Email - info@alphaedis.com

Contents

Exodium for All Americans

I hope the American people will be interested with the information I have just brought from my native country. I am writing the story of my trip to Lithuania and return at the suggestion of some of my fellow citizens, to whom I have narrated some ideas of it, in which they took much interest as instructive information for anyone who prepares for a trip to any part of the world. As this country is composed of citizens and patriots of all nationalities, so every citizen may get attraction to visit his native land; and even those who are born in this country are sometimes tempted to visit the country of their fathers and forefathers.

Exodium for Waterbury, Conn., Citizens Only.

My Dear Friends and Fellow Citizens:

I am glad to be with you again. Why am I glad? Because of the thirty-six years since I came to America, most of the time I have spent in Waterbury. Here I have lived for twenty-one years. Because in Waterbury I had time enough to make many friends, and if I did not do so, it is my own fault. In a word, in Waterbury my adopted citizenship must have rooted much deeper than in the other parts of the United States in which I have lived for a much shorter time.

What I Saw in Lithuania

No matter how zealous patriots we may become in our adopted country, we should not forget altogether our native country. As I did not venture to visit Lithuania under the czar in 1910, when I was visiting other parts of Europe, I had a great desire to see my native land after the horrible war. Anyone would be anxious to visit his native country after thirty-six years' absence.

It was not an easy task for me to get a passport, as the United States government objected to letting me cross Germany. There being no American consul to Germany, our government would not take the responsibility of protecting me in that country. To avoid crossing Germany I was advised to ask for a passport through Denmark, Switzerland and Libow, which I did. But the consul at Denmark refused to put the visa on my passport unless I would send a cable to Denmark and get the consent of the government. I went to Washington to see the ambassador of Denmark personally, and he told me the same as the consul in New York. I then went to the State Department asking to have a change made in my passport which would permit me to go through France. This the State Department refused to do. Finally I went to Mr. Walsh, the Senator from Massachusetts, who sent his secretary with me to the State Department, and the change was made immediately. I then went to the French ambassador who put his visa on my passport, and I was ready to go by way of France. It took me about two months to get the passport.

On August 30th, 1919, I embarked from New York, West Fourteenth Street, on the ship Transatlantique La Lorraine, to Havre, France. The second night of my trip was very foggy. Our ship sounded fog horns all night. I felt that the ship was standing still and went on deck to see what had happened. I saw lights flashing in two places, as if two ships were sinking not far from each other. On making inquiry from the sailors I found that our ship had collided with a fishing boat from Canada, cutting it in two. Fortunately all the fishermen were saved by our ship. I saw them struggling in their small boats against the waves near our ship, till they came close and the ropes were let down, by means of which their small boats were pulled up to our ship and the men were saved. Next day a collection for the fishermen was taken up among our passengers which amounted to 3000 francs, and they were carried to Havre.

All the voyage to France was very stormy except one day at the beginning and one day near France. Eight days' trip from New York to Havre. Sunday night about eight o'clock we reached Havre, but we were obliged to sleep on the ship because Monday morning the inspectors came to examine all passports and luggage. It was after one o'clock in the afternoon when I reached Paris, where I called at the Lithuanian Legation to get directions for going by way of Switzerland and Libow to Lithuania. They directed me to cross Germany, assuring me that two Lithuanian priests just before me had crossed Germany without any trouble. They were ignorant of the fact that one of those priests lost in Germany two suit cases valued at about five hundred dollars. This priest told me this later, when I met him in Lithuania.

After remaining in Paris for three days, trusting the advice of the Lithuanian Legation, having seen all authorities of France and England, I started for Lithuania by way of Belgium, Cologne, Berlin, Eytkunen, to the first station of Lithuania, called Valkaviskis. My baggage was addressed by the same route and was carried on the same train. The train left Paris at 9:30 P. M. I had a chance to see some of the ruined cities of Belgium only in the morning—at night there was no possibility of seeing. When we came to the first station in Germany, Herbesthal, the German inspector of passports and baggage came to examine all trunks. I was told that the train would wait there at the station till all the trunks were carried back to the baggage room and the same train would carry them together with the passengers. But it was just to the contrary. When I returned from the station after unlocking and locking my trunk the train was gone, and my trunk was left in Herbesthal and my two suit cases were carried away to Cologne. I was obliged to take another train to Cologne. On the first train we were supposed to arrive in Cologne about 11:00 a. m.; on the second train we did not arrive until very near four p. m. I was afraid of losing both my suit case, portable altar and the trunk. The suit case and the portable altar I found in Cologne, with the help of the British soldiers, but my trunk, worth about five hundred dollars, is lost forever in Germany.

In Cologne I tried in vain to get breakfast about 4:30 p. m. If you do not drink beer you can get nothing to eat. Those who drink beer get some herrings without bread. Bread you get only once a day—two small thin slices, for supper. There are no dining rooms on the trains any more in Germany.

At 9:30 p. m. the train left Cologne for Berlin. Near Berlin the British inspector of passports told me: "I allow you this time to pass this way to Lithuania if you promise me not to return to America the same way." I said: "I will return by way of Libow." At 8:30 a. m. the train arrived in Berlin and left for Koenigsberg and Eytkunen at 9:30 p. m. The evening trip from Berlin was a regular torture to me which I shall never forget. It seems to me that on that evening there must have been some sort of revolution among the German parties. No matter what the classification of the ticket of any passenger, whether first, second, third or fourth class, there was no distinction in the service on the train. There was such a multitude of people flocking to the train, the stronger ones trampling over the weaker—especially the women. Even after the train was filled there were many left to stand and wait for another train. I had a second class ticket and was obliged to sit in the corridor on my suit case all night and the greater part of the day.

On the train were many armed German soldiers going to Latvia and a part of Lithuania. I heard them talking about

Littau and Mittau Shauliai. After we passed Koeningsburg near the Eytkunen limit of Lithuania, some persons, one of them in the uniform of a soldier, began to speak the Lithuanian language. I asked them who they were and they told me they were Lithuanian officials returning from Berlin.

As soon as we arrived at Eytkunen, the German inspector asked to see our passports, and seeing on mine no visa by the German authority, I was told to return to Berlin for the necessary signature. I informed him that the consul of Switzerland in New York put the visa on my passport, permitting me to cross Germany. This was not sufficient as the Swiss consul had lost this authority at the termination of the war. Fortunately the Lithuanians whom I met at Eytkunen appealed to the Mayor of Virbalis, a city of Lithuania, who came to Eytkunen and obtained my release.

What a joy it was when a German soldier came to me while I was preparing to return to Berlin and told me to proceed to Lithuania. He led me to the train leaving for Vilkaviskis.

I was very anxious to see that part of the country for I was well acquainted with it thirty-six years ago. I saw that Lithuania is more devastated than Belgium. The Germans crossed through Belgium once only, while Lithuania had been the regular battlefield for the German and Russian armies. It was alternately captured and recaptured by the contending armies. When the Russian army was fleeing it destroyed whatever opportunity afforded, likewise the German army in its retreat carried everything in its wake, pillaged, burned and destroyed whatever it could not take. I noticed in particular one village which had been, only a few trees were visible. Numerous farm houses had been destroyed and burned to the ground. People now live in huts made partly of straw, old boards and clay. Not only the war, but nature has made changes in Lithuania. Rivers, such as the Seimena and Sirvinta, are only brooks. As we approached Vilkaviskis, my native town, the passengers called my attention to the station. My imagination failed to picture the rudely constructed hut as the same station of former years, which had been entirely destroyed by the invading army.

When I descended from the train, my sister's son-in-law, whom I had seen in Germany ten years ago, recognized me and conducted me to his home nearby. After spending a few happy hours with my friends and relatives I proceeded to the rectory. The next morning I was fortunate indeed to say mass for the first time in the church in which I was baptized. That afternoon at a meeting of the Lithuanian Sales Corporation, I lectured on American Lithuanians and Americans in general. Monday I went to Kaunas, or Kovno, to meet the [A]President of Lithuania, Anthony Smetona, to extend to him the congratulations of the Lithuanian Total Abstinence Organization of America.

[A] When I presented to the president of Lithuania, Mr. Anthony Smetona, the said recommendation of the Lithuanian Total Abstinence Organization in America, which is indeed a suggestion to introduce the prohibition of the manufacture and sale of intoxicating drinks in Lithuania—in other words, to imitate the American government in this respect, he expressed himself sufficiently in favor of it, but it is quite self-evident that he, as the President of Lithuania alone, cannot accomplish it. In our conversation he made a suggestion to me that I should strive to get a chance to speak publicly in Kaunas and in other places as much as possible on the subject of total abstinence, to which I expressed my hope that some of the priests of Kaunas, no doubt, would give me a chance there. Then the President said to me: "I have read in the Lithuanian American newspapers so much of you as the apostle of total abstinance among Lithuanians in America, I wish you would do the same here." In Lithuania the opportunity to speak to the people is offered only on Sunday, and in that case it is better in the church. So I had an opportunity on Sundays and delivered sermons in seven churches. In one a good number of priests as guests were assembled and listened to my sermon. They were pleased and at dinner table were discussing about

American prohibition. A great many of them are boldly opposed to it; some even expressing their doubt about total abstinance. But they all were curious to know what those Lithuanians will do who were arrested and punished for manufacturing at home and selling intoxicants without the license of the government, after hearing of that sermon in the church. Lithuanians in Lithuania have learned from the Germans when they were in occupation, not only how to make intoxicants, but also soap, sugar, etc.

At first I considered it might be an insult to speak about total abstinance in Lithuania, after the horrible war; that those people could not get any attraction to intoxicants having witnessed such horrors of the war. But I was soon informed by some good souls of the necessity of total abstinance and of the dangers and temptations of many to intoxication. So I could not part with Lithuania without making an effort to sow the seed that might produce some good effects in the field of total abstinance.

As soon as I came to Boston and Worcester the Lithuanian Total Abstinance Central Committee held its quarter-annual convention and caught me unexpectedly and cross-examined me on the situation in Lithuania. I was obliged to give an account of all I had done in Lithuania for total abstinance and prohibition. I told them that the President alone could not introduce prohibition, and that they will wait until a general convention of Lithuanians will take place. Then they appointed me to write to the President for an official answer to their communication, and that I should strive to find some way by which the Total Abstinance Organization of America could unite in co-operation with the same organization in Lithuania. So I undertook to do so, and am trying now to perform my obligation, but at present the correspondence with Lithuania is very slow.

The President of Lithuania was very thankful to the Americans and Lithuanians for the help they so generously extended to alleviate the sufferings of the people committed to his care. I visited the institution for teachers, called "Saules Namai", the Home of the Sun, which was almost miraculously saved from the devastations of war. While speaking of this institution I must also say a few words about the vast difference in spirit of the Lithuanians of the past and present. In former years the parents were free to send or not to send their children to school under the regime of the Czar. Few parents grasped this opportunity for they despised education, saying our forefathers were very good people without education, so we and our children will remain without it. I was very much surprised to see the spirit among the Lithuanians today. The young and old are eager to learn, to educate, to build schools and institutions of learning. The larger cities have gymnasiums or higher schools for girls and boys. They are creating new organizations to support these institutions and are exerting to the utmost to preserve them.

The Spirit of Patriotism

I would not dare to undertake to describe to you the spirit of patriotism of the Lithuanians in their native land, for I am a Lithuanian, and some may say that it is quite natural to praise one's own. But what I have heard from their enemies, the Germans, would seem to be legitimate. Even they are amazed to see the patriotic spirit of the Lithuanians, especially young boys eighteen and nineteen years of age who are so anxious to defend their liberty. They are presenting themselves in great numbers to the officials of the present government to be enrolled in the army, but for the lack of ammunition and clothing great numbers are turned away. In my conversation with some of these soldiers I asked them if they really thought they could defend their country from the yoke of their oppressors. Their answer was: "We will not submit to any yoke; we know well that our fathers and forefathers suffered for so many centuries, and we in turn shall defend our liberty to the last drop of blood." One of these soldiers was preparing to return to war against the Kolchakians and Germans, to expel them from the city called Siauliai, which they had lately occupied. After repulsing the Bolshevik from the Dvinsk, they had a few weeks' rest and then marched to Kaunas.

At the time I was visiting Lithuania she was surrounded by enemies—on the north and east by the Bolsheviks, on the west by Kolchak and the insurgent Germans, and on the south by the Poles. The most stupendous fact is that at present the Poles are the most dangerous foes of the Lithuanians. The Poles, rejoicing in their own liberation from the yoke of oppression, are altogether unmindful that they are striving to place the Lithuanian nation under worse oppression. When the Germans occupied Lithuania they did not treat them as roughly as the Poles are doing at this moment. For example, I was in Lithuania when the Poles took Seinai, the seat of Bishop Karosas, which is a Lithuanian city, imprisoned the Lithuanian Bishop in his residence, expelled the ecclesiastical students from their seminary, arrested two priests and carried them to Poland. If any of the remaining priests are called out on a sick call, they send armed soldiers to accompany the priest and guard his movements strictly. They did not permit the Bishop to correspond with his pastors, or the priests of the diocese, nor was anyone permitted to call on him. The Germans during their occupation never guarded a priest going to sick calls.

Here is a translation of a little article taken from a Lithuanian political daily newspaper called Lietuva (Lithuania) of October 10, 1919:

"Actions of the Polish Occupants.—The Polish army came to the district of Vilkaviskis in September. After two weeks they began to show their rapacity. They robbed Augustin Kliogutis of Norvydai while he was going home from church, with five other companions, stripped them of their clothing and left them in puris naturalibus."

Similar notices filled the paper with the various robberies committed by soldiers of the Polish army. On September 21, 1919, one of the Polish officials called the Lithuanian people together and promised them great favors—while the people asked him to stop the robberies, which would have been the greatest favor possible. The Lithuanians say: "If the Poles could grant us favors they would not keep their soldiers half naked and half starved."

For all this greediness and avariciousness of the Polish people I do not blame the good Polish citizens and patriots, because in our days in all nationalities there are a great many political parties, of which the governments are composed, the greater number of those compelling the entire nation to act against the good will of the citizens. On the other hand we Lithuanians cannot boast too much of our patriotism, as though we had no traitor, even among the Poles. There are many Polonized Lithuanians, or so-called Poles who by the familiar and long intercourse with the Polish race, gradually neglected and despised and finally rejected entirely the Lithuanian language, adopted the Polish language in such a manner that some of them do not acknowledge to be Lithuanians but claim to be of Polish descendency—in other words, Polish by birth. These are the greatest persecutors of the Lithuanians now. This is the principal reason why the Poles took possession of Vilna, the first capitol of Lithuania. They maintain that all the province of Vilna is purely Polish. In this way the Polish patriots, joined by the Polonized Lithuanian renegades and traitors, try to induce others to join their party, and to struggle to find the demarkation between the two countries would appear endless without the final decision of the allies.

It is true what the Rev. Laukaitis remarked in his speech, that the Poles are carrying on their propaganda to induce more of the Lithuanian farmers, ignorant enough, to sign the Polish alliance. They send their crafty speakers to the villages near the boundary trying to persuade the Lithuanian government to permit a ballot to be cast in Vilna as to which side they prefer to belong. These propagandists do not tell the truth. They, like the Bolsheviks, promise mountains of gold, and in the end give bitter sorrow. It would indeed be foolish to allow a ballot after these speakers obtain the signatures of the farmers, who, through their ignorance, are misled by the vain promises and misleading arguments that the Lithuanians are incapable of self-government, without first hearing our side. With such arguments it would take only a few months to lead astray all the Lithuanians or vice versa Lithuanian speakers could bring to our side all Poles.

Members of the British mission at Kaunas (Kovo) told me that the Lithuanians are very brave soldiers who have so many enemies, yet nevertheless keep their spirit of patriotism so long and so firmly. It stands to reason then, that the Lithuanians, as a nation, are very brave, considering the numbers of Poles and Lithuanians, you could hardly imagine how the Lithuanians could dare oppose the Poles, and yet you see they attempt to oppose many armies. Lithuania has about one-fifth the population of Poland in Europe and about one-third the population of the Poles in America.

While I was spending five days in Kaunas, the temporary capital of Lithuania, the President received a cable from Lloyd George, London, recognizing the independence of Lithuania. This was on the night of September 26th. As soon as the cable arrived the Lithuanian government had the greatest demonstration in the history of the nation, wholly unmindful of the weather and rain. Parades, speeches, and the wildest rejoicing for this newly realized dream took possession of the city.

I intended to remain in Lithuania until May, but was obliged to change my mind for more than one reason. My winter apparel was in the lost baggage in Germany and the cold weather was approaching rapidly. There was no possibility for me to visit all the Parish churches as intended. There was no means of travel, train or vehicle. During the war the Lithuanians were deprived of all their horses. Those which they have now are used on the farms. With the greatest difficulty I managed to visit the following: Kybartai, Virbalis, Alvitas, Lankeliskiai, Valkaviskis, Gizai, Marjampole, Kaunas, and Kamendulai. I did not get the opportunity to see the Bishop of Vilona; for there was no consul of Poland in Lithuania to sign my passport. I spoke with the suffragan of the bishop of Kaunas. The Bishop of Seinai was arrested by the Poles. The last and to me the most important reason why I was determined to return to America immediately was because of the bad treatment the Lithuanian Bishops, priests and ecclesiastical students received in Seinai. I resolved to return to appeal to the sympathetic hearts of the Americans to protest against the wrong-doings of the Poles.

After visiting the above mentioned places, I decided to find out when and how I could get a ship from England to New York. I went to Kaunas a second time, as I was advised that I should telephone to Libow for information with regard to sailings of English ships—so as to know how long I could remain in Lithuania.

At Kaunas I learned that the Germans and Kolchakians had taken Siauliai, a city between Kaunas and Libow, and that I could not go back to America by way of Libow. The telephone was interrupted by the occupants. Then there was no way left to me but to go to the English mission at Kaunas to get a permit to go back via Germany, and to go to the German consul at Kaunas to put a visa on my passport for the same purpose. Having obtained all the documents I said adieu to Kaunas, adieu Lithuania, adieu Vilkaviskis, adieu my sister and all her family. On October 16 I took the German train from Eytkunen to Berlin and Cologne. In Cologne I remained three days, making investigation for my lost baggage, but in vain. Via Brussells to Ostend, where I embarked on the four hours vessel from Ostend to Dower, an English port. On October 23 I came to London at 9:30 p. m. There I was obliged to spend all night walking up and down the front of the church to avoid catching cold, because there was no possibility of getting a place in any of the hotels. Next morning the first thing I went to find out how soon I could get the ship Mauretania. I was informed that it was not sure if the Mauretania would be able to start for New York on December 30, because it was in repair. There were some smaller ships to start sooner, which I did not risk. In Scotland two Lithuanian priests who were informed of my coming to London and would not be able to get a ship to America for a long time, invited me to Scotland to give mission to the Lithuanians there. Having consented to do so, I came to Glasgow November 5. In the following places I gave mission of four days each: Graigneuk, Motherwell, Garfin, Burnbank; and a whole week in each of the following places: Mossend and Glasgow. I also spent one week at Manchester in England. The missions were very successful in all places. The Lithuanians were rejoicing and saying that my not getting a ship was very providential. On December 21, I came back to London and bought my ticket to cross the ocean on the Canadian ship called Empress of France, which was to start January 3, 1920. On December 24 I came to Liverpool to spend a few days there in getting ready for my voyage to Canada and the United States. On coming to Liverpool, I learned that the "Empress of France" was to start four days later, than was intended, on January 7th.

The Lithuanian people of Liverpool asked me to give a Mission to them. On the Sunday after Christmas I opened a mission for the Lithuanians of Liverpool, and closed it the next Sunday.

On Wednesday, January 7th, I embarked on the ship for St. John, Canada. The "Empress of France" claims to make her trip in six days, but in rough weather it took us fully eight days, so it was January 15th, about 7:30 p. m., we arrived in St. John, Canada. Next morning, after examining our passports and trunks, we landed. There was no train to Boston, Mass., till 7:30 p. m. I arrived at Boston January 17th, just a few minutes before 12 o'clock a. m.

The Object of This Lecture.

Some one may inquire of me, what I wish the Americans to do for Lithuania?

All small nations of the world, so far, had the greatest confidence in the **League of Nations**, which promised to all equal liberty of existence and self-determination, toleration of its language, etc. The principal characteristic of any nation is the language of that nation. If the native language is forbidden to any nation by those becoming its conquerors, the nation is exterminated.

All the enemies of Lithuania seem to be very anxious to deprive the people of their language, for as soon as they take possession of some of the Lithuanian cities or towns, the first step they take is to forbid the children to be taught the Lithuanian language. Now, with all the smaller nations of the world, Lithuanians are crying: "Where is Justice? Why are our enemies so anxious to deprive us of our language? In what respect is our enemies' language better than our own? Is it our fault that we are born of Lithuanian parents and speak Lithuanian language?"

Philologists are demonstrating that the Lithuanian language, of all European languages, is the nearest to Sanscrit. All educated people are glad to know that there is some nation in existence using the oldest of speaking tongues. Why is it that, in our days, people who claim to be very highly educated are attempting to exterminate the nation which is using the oldest language? Nothing but envy, greed and grab!

Now, as the **League or Nations** is gradually dying, so all hope of preserving the Lithuanian nation, together with its language, is diminishing.

Some people maintain that the **League of Nations** is diametrically opposed to the will of God, expressed in the prophesies of the Bible; that there will be no end of wars to the very end of the world. But we know, positively, that God does not want wars; that God wants peace. We know very well that all the causes of the wars are to be found in the iniquities of men—in the seven capital sins. If not all the prophesies of the Bible, at least a great many can be explained conditionally.

If people mend their behaviour, the punishments, which have been foretold for their crimes, will not take place, because the nature itself, which has been so directed by the Creator to punish man for deviating from the order, is changed by man's actions. In fact, some of the prophesies of the Old Testament we could not explain, save in this way. If all people would strive to stop the wars, the **League of Nations** would become the means of bringing universal peace on earth, according to the will of the Almighty. I wish the American people would study this question as closely as possible, and bring all nations to everlasting peace.

We can plainly see, from the following text of the Bible, that God wants all people to live in peace always: "But if one strike thee on thy right cheek, turn to him also the other. * * * And if any man will contend with thee in judgment, and take away thy coat, let go thy cloak also unto him."—Matt. v. 40. God could never have said this, unless He foresaw the possibility of lasting peace among all men and all nations in this world.

Just imagine, if all people and all nations in this world were readily prepared to turn their other cheek to the one who is ready to strike you on your right cheek. It is self evident there would be none to strike his neighbor on his right cheek. And if everybody in the world would be ready to let go his cloak to one who is ready to take away his coat, there would be none to deprive any one of his coat. As long as we believe that Jesus Christ, who said these words, is true God and true man; as long as we know that every man has free will, and can do what he pleases, so long is this principle possible to every man. Even to those people who do not believe in the divinity of Jesus Christ, this principle could be explained as a natural law: Do not do unto others what you do not want others to do unto you; do unto others what you wish others to do unto you. If all intelligent people, together with those who are aspiring to a higher education, would strive to organize a league to educate all people in this particular principle, there would be no doubt of its success, because no people would desire to have another war. Everybody knows that war does no good to any one; and that another war would be ten times worse than the one we have had. I do not see why the **League of Nations** or another similar reorganized regulation of nations, should not attract all nations to a union of such principles as these.

The objector insists: "I do not mean that the **League of Nations** is opposed to the will of God, as if God wanted wars, but God, foreseeing the wickedness of men, prophesied that there will be no peace among men to the end of the world."

It is sufficient to us to know that God does not want war, that God wants peace; or, in other words, to know God's will, and to strive to do it. As long as we know that either the **League of Nations** or other international organization is in accordance to the will of God—who is striving to induce all nations to prevent wars in future—just as God wants all people to live in peace always—so we ought to strive, by word and example, to induce all nations to hate wars and live in peace. As every human being has a right to existence, so every family and every nation has a right to exist and use its own language, etc. No one has the right to destroy small nations because they are too small to govern themselves. For the very reason, if there be no more wars, if the **League of Nations** is to be sincere in every respect, to reject all greediness, which is the cause of wars, there would be no more necessity of greatness to be able to defend against foes. Just as every family is capable of governing itself, so the smallest nation can govern itself.

So far the League of Nations does not produce its desired effect, because there is no confidence in some nations in one another. One nation does not trust the other. It is a new branch of science. It requires a good deal of study—and study by all nations and all persons—until some one may discover the means to induce the desired confidence satisfactory for all nations. I hope Americans will make the greatest progress in this line, as in everything else.

My opinion is that all nations could be induced to trust one another, if the above principle of natural law would be plainly explained, either in all languages or in **Aspiranto** language. If all representatives of all nations would sign the agreement, then the danger would be removed far away. If it is so difficult to induce one nation to trust the other nation to join the League, how can you expect any small nation to be inspired with any confidence when it is annexed to another greater nation by force? No matter how long it will be annexed, it will seek opportunity to free itself, and, unless you amputate its tongue, it will adhere to its language. Just exactly like a cat and a dog in one bag, one will bark, the other will cry its own song, or, like a patched dress, will remain patched forever.

Milton Keynes UK
Ingram Content Group UK Ltd.
UKHW041909120324
439302UK00005B/408